RUMORS OF WAR

KENNETH COPELAND

Harrison House
Tulsa, Oklahoma

Rumors of War—Finding Peace and Protection in Troubled Times

ISBN 0-88114-832-6   KC-832-6   30-0045

All scripture is from the following translation:

King James Version (KJV)

Reprinted 2000

Published by Harrison House, Inc.
P.O. Box 35035
Tulsa, Oklahoma 74153

Rumors of War
Finding Peace and Protection
in Troubled Times

If there was ever a generation where people needed to know how to enter into God's protection and stay there, it's this generation.

We face harm and harassment at every turn. People drive down the street shooting guns through the walls of houses. Wars and rumors of wars are commonplace news. There's the drug war. There's violence in South America and the African nations. Then there's the Middle East. It's literally all over the globe, staring us in the face.

Most people react to the danger in one of two ways. They either get calloused to it and ignore it...or they simply wring their hands and moan, "Dear God, help us." But neither one of those ways will get us through. Ignoring the problems won't make them go away and, frankly, neither will our helpless cries of despair.

We have to deal with the dangers around us. Whether it feels good or not. Whether it looks pretty or not. We have a part to play in them.

Jesus Himself knew we were going to have to face times like these. He warned us about them in Matthew 24:4-6. There He said, *"Take heed that no man deceive you. For many shall come in my name, saying, I am Christ; and shall deceive many. And ye shall hear of wars and rumours of wars: see that ye be not troubled."*

See that ye be not troubled. That's what Jesus said we should do when we go through dangerous times. When we hear of wars and rumors of wars, we're not to let it cripple our faith and throw us into

4

anxiety. We're to refuse to let that trouble enter into our hearts.

We're also to guard against deception. *"Take heed,"* Jesus said, *"that no man deceive you."* You know, these days everyone has something to say about what's happening. The news media. The politicians. Your next-door neighbor. Everybody! Even though those people don't intend to deceive you, they're looking at things through the world's eyes instead of through the eyes of the Word of God.

If you'll let him, Satan will use them to fill your mind with worries. He'll use the media to bring to you all the terrors of war. To show you every kind of horrible thing you can think of. Why? To stir up hate and fear inside you. To deceive you into abandoning your faith and letting fear fill your heart.

He creates wars outside you so that he can gain access to your insides. If it stays outside you, it won't accomplish his objective. He has to deceive you into opening your heart and mind and letting it in.

But you can guard against that by taking heed! By paying attention to what God is saying instead of what the world is saying. By concentrating on Him, looking at things through His eyes.

That means, whether you're the one who's facing danger or the one at home praying for a loved one who's facing it—you have to lock into God's Word and stay there. It doesn't matter what's on television. It doesn't matter what's in the newspapers. Your future isn't based on that. Your future will be determined by your faith in God's Word.

But I'll tell you right up front, it takes real commitment to keep your attention on that Word when violence is breaking out all around you, because that violence is specifically designed by the devil to distract you from it. Let me show you what I mean. For years, there have been prophecies about a great and mighty revival that would come at the end of this 20th century. Sure enough, we're beginning to see the evidence of it around us. During a recent Southwest Believers' Convention, we experienced such an amazing outpouring of the Spirit that every person there realized we'd stepped across the threshold of that revival. We knew that it had begun.

Strangely, it was that very week that the incidents in the Middle East exploded quite suddenly. "What's happening here?" I asked the Lord. "What is this?"

He showed me that whenever He pours out His best in a mighty display of power, people get healed and saved and delivered and encouraged and set free from the bondages that have held them. We call that outpouring "revival" and when it comes, Satan tries to counter it by pouring out his "best." His best takes the form of relentless destruction, maiming, crippling disease and death. In its ultimate manifestation, we call that "war."

All through history, and particularly during this century, the revival of God has paralleled war. We've seen mighty outpourings of God during this 20th century, and at the same time, we've also seen mankind's most terrible wars.

Those wars have actually been Satan's specific attempt to sidetrack us, to take our attention off the outpouring of God and center us up on war instead. It's a diversionary tactic whose sole purpose is to stop the move of God.

How do we keep from falling prey to it? How do we keep from falling into the fear and deception Jesus warned us about?

Settle the Victory in Your Heart

First of all, we have to come to the complete and absolute decision that *we are the victors*. The victory is ours and the battle is the Lord's. We must settle that within ourselves.

It's imperative that we do whatever we have to do to get that into our spirits. We must stay in the Word; take communion every 30 minutes if necessary; fellowship with the Lord until confidence in Him rises up within us and chases out every thought of failure and defeat. Not only for us as individuals, but for us as a nation.

Let me tell you something. After Jesus defeated the devil and left the earth, the Bible says He sat down at the right hand of the Father. He sat down expecting all His enemies to be made His footstool (Acts 2:34-35). Do you understand what that means?

It means Jesus is not standing up wringing His hands. He's seated, confident in His victory. So you and I need to start acting that way too. We need to talk and act like Jesus has actually taken authority over the devil and his bunch.

We shouldn't go around crying and acting like He never went to the Cross. We shouldn't scream and carry on and wait for somebody to come get the devil off us.

No! We need to act as though Jesus has already won. As far as He's concerned, it's done. So we need to learn to act as though it's done as far as we're concerned too.

We need to say, "Thank You, Lord! Praise You, Jesus!" and tell the devil, "You take your dirty hands off me and my loved ones. Don't you realize that Jesus is seated on the right hand of the Father?"

Remember this: You don't look up at the devil, you look down at him. He's under your feet!

Is it possible to have that kind of confidence in the midst of the kinds of threats we're facing right now? Yes! The Word of God says so. In Psalm 112, it says that the man who fears the Lord and delights greatly in His commandments *"shall not be afraid of evil tidings: his heart is fixed, trusting in the Lord. His heart is established, he shall not be afraid, until he see his desire upon his enemies"* (verses 7-8).

That kind of person is locked in. He's sure that the victory is his. Once you have that kind of assurance, nothing—not even wars and rumors of wars—will be able to move you.

Speak Out Your Deliverance

The second thing we need to do to keep from falling into Satan's trap is to speak out loud about the deliverance of the Lord. Psalm 91:2-3 says, *"I will say of the Lord, He is my refuge and my fortress: my God; in him will I trust. Surely he shall deliver [me]...."*

Notice that scripture doesn't say, "He will deliver me and then I'll go everywhere telling about it." No, it says, I'll *say* it and *then,* in response to what I've said, He will deliver me.

That's not just some super-spiritual idea either. It works. I know one soldier who, during World War II, survived a bombing raid by huddling underneath a bunk bed shouting out Psalm 91. By the time that raid was over, the bombs had destroyed the building he was in and everything in it, except that one little bed sitting right out in the middle of the room.

I have a close friend who did that same thing all through the time he fought in Vietnam. He was in hard infantry with guys falling around him left and right. But all the time, day and night, he held onto that 91st Psalm, saying right out loud, *"A thousand shall fall at thy side, and ten thousand at thy right hand; but it shall not come nigh thee"* (verse 7).

For two years he fought in the worst places with unbelievable danger all around him. But he was protected. He said of the Lord, "He is my refuge and my fortress. He is my God, in Him will I trust. Surely, He shall deliver me!"

You can do the same thing those soldiers did. Take hold of that 91st Psalm. Say it to yourself so often that you absolutely know it by heart. Just go around muttering it again and again.

Romans 10:17 says faith comes by hearing, and hearing by the Word of God. When you speak the Word of God to yourself, your spirit hears it, and the more you hear it, the more your faith grows. So, keep on speaking God's Word of protection and eventually your faith in that protection will become so strong nothing will be able to shake it.

"Well, I don't know, Brother Copeland. That sounds like a lot of work."

You're right. It *is* a lot of work. But, that's what it takes to walk in the protection of

God. It doesn't just come automatically. True, He's already provided it through His Word and it's there for each one of us, but it's not going to leap on us from behind. We have to believe for it on a consistent basis or we'll miss it.

You see, even though the Word of God is powerful, even though it's sharper than a two-edged sword, it can't do anything for you until you activate it. I don't care how many times you've heard the Word preached or how many times you've read it, God says, until you mix it with faith, it profits you nothing! (Hebrews 4:2)

God's Word contains the most powerful promises of protection on the face of the earth and it carries within itself the power to fulfill those promises. Yet it won't do a thing in your life about protecting you until you make it the foundation of your faith.

It's like salvation. God has already provided it for anyone who will believe for it, act on it and receive it. But we have to use our faith to get in on it—and like it or not, faith is labor. It's not some passive state you slide into accidentally. The book of Hebrews says we labor to enter into that rest of faith (Hebrews 4:11). We don't labor to fix the problem. We labor to enter into our rest with God.

What does that labor include? Sometimes it includes getting up out of your chair and turning off the TV and saying, "I'm not watching the world's news anymore. I'm tired of seeing this conflict through their eyes." It includes getting out your Bible and saying, "I believe that. I don't care what anybody else says. I don't care what the situation looks like. I believe God's Word." It includes putting your faith first and protecting your mind instead of flooding it all the time with the things of the world.

Some people are afraid if they turned off the TV and buried their nose in the Bible, they'd be caught off guard by world events and they'd be unequipped to handle them. But the truth is, they'd be *more* equipped to handle them than ever before.

You see, the primary battles aren't taking place here on the earth where you can see them and hear them. They're taking place in the heavenlies. They're spiritual battles and you can't fight spiritual battles from a natural perspective. You have to get God's perspective. You have to put the spirit realm first.

What's more, the Bible says when you fight in the spirit realm, you don't fight against flesh and blood, but against principalities, powers, rulers of the darkness of this world and spiritual wickedness in high places—and the weapon you use to fight with is the Word. Ephesians 6 calls it the "sword of the Spirit" and it will fight the fight if you'll put it out there.

Follow the Rules of Faith

The third thing that will help you avoid the dangers the devil is trying to lure you into is this: Follow the rules of faith. In 1 Timothy 2:1-2, the Holy Spirit instructs us to offer *"first of all, supplications, prayers, intercessions, and giving of thanks...for all men; for kings, and for all that are in authority."* That means we're to pray not only for the good guys, but for the bad guys too.

If we're going to successfully fight this fight of faith, we're going to have to obey God's guidelines. We can't jump up and start ranting and raving about what a maniac somebody is.

Pay attention now. I don't care what dictator is doing what, keep your mouth shut and quit speaking out against him. Don't sing ugly songs about him or make up stupid jokes.

Do what Proverbs 4 says and protect your heart against foolishness like that *"with all diligence."* I don't care how you feel about it. I don't care if your flesh rears up and gets mad. Put it back down and fight that battle in the heavenlies. Fight it with prayer and the Word, and keep your faith strong by guarding yourself against hate.

Hate will cripple your faith. It will cripple the power of God in you, and you'll lose the spiritual ability to do what's necessary to protect the lives of those who depend on your faith.

That same thing holds true when you're actually the one doing the fighting. It doesn't matter whether you're in the cockpit of a fighter plane or in a foxhole with a rifle in your hand or engaged in hand-to-hand conflict—you have to keep your faith first and stay out of hate.

You can't let hate for the man that's trying to kill you get inside of you. Even in a combat situation, the devil can't get to you if you're abiding by the rules of faith, covering your mind with the Word and declaring the mercy of God. That was one of the secrets of David's success as a combat soldier. He fought his battles with God's power first and then his weapon—sword or stone and sling—either one, backed by faith, could not be defeated.

Listen, my friend. No matter how much we try to ignore it...or how despairingly we cry about it, trouble *is* coming. It's constantly out there, and it's heading right toward you every day just like Jesus said it would.

But don't let that trouble trouble you! Instead, chase doubt out and settle the victory in your heart. Speak out the delivering power of the Lord and follow the rules of faith. You will surely see the salvation of God!

Prayer for Salvation
and Baptism in the Holy Spirit

Heavenly Father, I come to You in the Name of Jesus. Your Word says, *"Whosoever shall call on the name of the Lord shall be saved"* (Acts 2:21). I am calling on You. I pray and ask Jesus to come into my heart and be Lord over my life, according to Romans 10:9-10: *"If thou shalt confess with thy mouth the Lord Jesus, and shalt believe in thine heart that God hath raised him from the dead, thou shalt be saved. For with the heart man believeth unto righteousness; and with the mouth confession is made unto salvation."* I do that now. I confess that Jesus is Lord, and I believe in my heart that God raised Him from the dead.

I am now reborn! I am a Christian—a child of Almighty God! I am saved! You also said in Your Word, *"If ye then, being evil, know how to give good gifts unto your children:* HOW MUCH MORE *shall your heavenly Father give the Holy Spirit to them that ask him?"* (Luke 11:13). I'm also asking You to fill me with the Holy Spirit. Holy Spirit, rise up within me as I praise God. I fully expect to speak with other tongues as You give me utterance (Acts 2:4).

Begin to praise God for filling you with the Holy Spirit. Speak those words and syllables you receive—not in your own language, but the language given to you by the Holy Spirit. You have to use your own voice. God will not force you to speak. Worship and praise Him in your heavenly language—in other tongues.

Continue with the blessing God has given you and pray in tongues each day.

You are a born-again, Spirit-filled believer. You'll never be the same!

Find a good Word of God preaching church, and become a part of a church family who will love and care for you as you love and care for them.

We need to be hooked up to each other. It increases our strength in God. It's God's plan for us.

About the Author

For more than 32 years, Kenneth Copeland has led countless believers on a journey to maturity in the principles of faith, love, healing, prosperity, redemption and righteousness. Through the Believers Voice of Victory broadcast—one of the top five Neilsen-rated inspirational programs—and BVOV Magazine, he has brought revelation knowledge on the truths of God's Word. He has taught Christians everywhere that they can conquer the problems and challenges life brings through faith in God's Word.

Books Available from
Kenneth Copeland Ministries

by Kenneth Copeland
* A Ceremony of Marriage
  A Matter of Choice
  Covenant of Blood
  Faith and Patience—The Power Twins
* Freedom From Fear
  Giving and Receiving
  Honor—Walking in Honesty, Truth and Integrity
  How to Conquer Strife
  How to Discipline Your Flesh
  How to Receive Communion
  Living at the End of Time—A Time of Supernatural Increase
  Love Never Fails
  Managing God's Mutual Funds
* Now Are We in Christ Jesus
* Our Covenant With God
* Prayer—Your Foundation for Success
  Prosperity: The Choice Is Yours
  Rumors of War
* Sensitivity of Heart
  Six Steps to Excellence in Ministry
  Sorrow Not! Winning Over Grief and Sorrow
* The Decision Is Yours
* The Force of Faith
* The Force of Righteousness
  The Image of God in You
  The Laws of Prosperity
* The Mercy of God
  The Miraculous Realm of God's Love
  The Outpouring of the Spirit—The Result of Prayer
* The Power of the Tongue
  The Power to Be Forever Free
  The Troublemaker
* The Winning Attitude
  Turn Your Hurts Into Harvests
* Welcome to the Family
* You Are Healed!
  Your Right-Standing With God

by Gloria Copeland
* And Jesus Healed Them All
  Are You Ready?
  Build Your Financial Foundation
  Build Yourself an Ark
  Fight On!
  God's Prescription for Divine Health
  God's Success Formula
  God's Will for You
  God's Will for Your Healing
  God's Will is Prosperity
* God's Will Is the Holy Spirit
* Harvest of Health
  Hidden Treasures
  Living Contact
* Love—The Secret to Your Success

No Deposit—No Return
Pleasing the Father
Pressing In—It's Worth It All
Shine On!
The Power to Live a New Life
The Unbeatable Spirit of Faith
* Walk in the Spirit
Walk With God
Well Worth the Wait

Books Co-Authored by Kenneth and Gloria Copeland
Family Promises
Healing Promises
Prosperity Promises
Protection Promises

From Faith to Faith—A Daily Guide to Victory
From Faith to Faith—A Perpetual Calendar

One Word From God Series
• One Word from God Can Change Your Destiny
• One Word from God Can Change Your Family
• One Word from God Can Change Your Finances
• One Word from God Can Change Your Formula for Success
• One Word from God Can Change Your Health
• One Word from God Can Change Your Nation
• One Word from God Can Change Your Prayer Life
• One Word from God Can Change Your Relationships

Over the Edge—A Youth Devotional
Over the Edge Xtreme Planner for Students—
  Designed for the School Year

Pursuit of His Presence—A Daily Devotional
Pursuit of His Presence—A Perpetual Calendar

Other Books Published by KCP
The First 30 Years—A Journey of Faith
  The story of the lives of Kenneth and Gloria Copeland
Real People. Real Needs. Real Victories.
  A book of testimonies to encourage your faith.

John G. Lake—His Life, His Sermons, His Boldness of Faith
The Holiest of All, by Andrew Murray
The New Testament in Modern Speech,
  by Richard Francis Weymouth

Products Designed for Today's Children and Youth
Baby Praise Board Book
Baby Praise Christmas Board Book
Noah's Ark Coloring Book
Shout! Super-Activity Book

Commander Kellie and the Superkids Adventure Novels
#1   Escape from Jungle Island
#2   In Pursuit of the Enemy
#3   Mysterious Presence, The
#4   Quest for the Second Half, The

SWORD Adventure Book

*Available in Spanish

World Offices
of Kenneth Copeland Ministries

For more information and a free catalog, please write the office nearest you.

Kenneth Copeland Ministries
Fort Worth, Texas 76192-0001

Kenneth Copeland
Locked Bag 2600
Mansfield Delivery Centre
QUEENSLAND 4122
AUSTRALIA

Kenneth Copeland
Post Office Box 15
BATH
BA1 1GD
ENGLAND U.K.

Kenneth Copeland
Private Bag X 909
FONTAINEBLEAU 2032
REPUBLIC OF SOUTH AFRICA

Kenneth Copeland
Post Office Box 378
SURREY, BC V3T 5B6
CANADA

UKRAINE
L'VIV 290000
Post Office Box 84
Kenneth Copeland
L'VIV 290000
UKRAINE

Learn more about Kenneth Copeland Ministries
by visiting our website at:
www.kcm.org

WE'RE HERE FOR YOU!

Believer's Voice of Victory Television Broadcast

Join Kenneth and Gloria Copeland, and the *Believer's Voice of Victory* broadcasts Monday through Friday and on Sunday each week, and learn how faith in God's Word can take your life from ordinary to extraordinary. This teaching from God's Word is designed to get you where you want to be—*on top!*

You can catch the *Believer's Voice of Victory* broadcast on your local, cable or satellite channels.

*Check your local listings for times and stations in your area.

Believer's Voice of Victory Magazine

Enjoy inspired teaching and encouragement from Kenneth and Gloria Copeland and guest ministers each month in the *Believer's Voice of Victory* magazine. Also included are real-life testimonies of God's miraculous power and divine intervention into the lives of people just like you!

It's more than just a magazine—it's a ministry.

Shout! . . . The dynamic magazine for kids!

Shout! The Voice of Victory for Kids is a Bible-charged, action-packed, bimonthly magazine available FREE to kids everywhere! Featuring Wichita Slim and Commander Kellie and the Superkids, *Shout!* is filled with colorful adventure comics, challenging games and puzzles, exciting short stories, solve-it-yourself mysteries and much more!!

Stand up, sign up and get ready to *Shout!*

To receive a FREE subscription to *Believer's Voice of Victory,* or to give a child you know a FREE subscription to *Shout!,* write:

Kenneth Copeland Ministries
Fort Worth, Texas 76192-0001
or call:
1-800-600-7395
(9 a.m.-5 p.m. CT)
Or visit our website at:
www.kcm.org

If you are writing from outside the U.S., please contact the KCM office nearest you. Addresses for all Kenneth Copeland Ministries offices are listed on the previous page.

The Harrison House Vision

Proclaiming the truth and the power
Of the Gospel of Jesus Christ
With excellence;

Challenging Christians to
Live victoriously,
Grow spiritually,
Know God intimately.